52 Leadership Ideas

You Can Use with Students

Projects that Pastors, Parents and Campus
Ministers Can Do with Their Students

Tim Elmore

*This book is dedicated to Kevin Miller:
a leader, a man who loves investing in the next
generation, and a father who is commited
to helping his kids become all they can be.
Thanks for your example, Kevin.*

Table of Contents

How to Get the Most Out of This Book

You don't have to read this book all the way through. That's the beauty of it. It is designed to be a small reference guide to you as a parent, teacher or campus worker. It is chalk full of ideas that are inexpensive, easy to pull off, and that teach some ingredient of leadership to the young person with whom you share them.

I've included fifty-two ideas. There is one for each week of the year. They are listed under ten categories. I suggest you select the young person you wish to invest in, then evaluate what they most need to learn about leadership. Is it people skills? Is it problem solving? How about vision? Once you pick the category, try one idea per week. Here's what I would do if I were you.

First, determine to do the idea *with* them. You are a tour guide not a travel agent. Don't just tell them what to do and where to go—go with them and do it together. You'll both be better for the experience, and you'll have more talking points afterward.

Second, prepare them for the experience. The ideas include field trips, interviews with leaders, exercises around the house, conversations around a TV show or video, and experiments with others in your community. Just in case you are more excited about teaching them leadership than they are to learn it, you'll want to talk with them and get them mentally ready for the time you spring it on them.

Third, keep a journal of your experiences together. Ask them to do it, too. This will enable you to chart their growth and record exactly what you were thinking and feeling along the way. Later, you can actually spot the improvements you both make.

Educators have confirmed that people learn 10% of what they hear; 50% of what they see, but 80% of what they experience first hand. Be sure you don't reduce this to a lecture on each subject. Gently push them to try the ideas themselves. You'll find that many of them are just plain fun, and will spark both great conversation as well as lots of laughter. Naturally, some of the ideas will work better for more mature students, while others are great for beginners on the leadership journey. Over the last year, these ideas have been tested with students from kindergarten to college.

My goal is that you will glorify God on the journey. Because the ideas are Christian in nature, they're designed to spark a greater love for God and for people. They're designed to expand the student's positive influence in this world. I believe you'll see great fruit from practicing these ideas. Jesus told us God is glorified by our fruit (John 15:8).

Long ago the Apostle Paul took a young man named Timothy and decided to build a leader out of him. He penned some words in his final letter to him, before he died. May this be our challenge as we invest in future generations:

"And the things which you have heard from me, in the presence of many witnesses, these entrust to faithful men who will be able to teach others also."   *(II Timothy 2:2)*

For more Information, contact us at:
www.growingleaders.com

Cultivating the Blessing

Cultivating the Blessing

Two years ago, our daughter Bethany turned thirteen. Prior to her birthday, we had already noticed signs of her becoming a teenager. There was a hint of an independent spirit; she had formed definite opinions on every topic; she requested a cell phone and a personal television for her room; public kisses from dad were embarrassing; and she was already shaving her legs! (Aren't girls supposed to wait until after they get married to do that?)

Because my wife, Pam, and I recognized the significance of this time in her life, we decided to do something to help her transition well into womanhood. In Jewish culture, young men and women experience a bar mitzvah or a bat mitzvah. These celebrations are designed to be a rite of passage into adulthood. In America, most of us have no such ceremony. Our closest event is getting a driver's license or high school diploma. Consequently, boys grow older, but often don't grow up. Girls want the privileges that come with age, but not the responsibilities that go with it. Pam and I decided to plan a significant year for Bethany that would enable her to be ready for a life of responsibility and leadership.

We sat down with Bethany, and selected six women whom we would ask to be one-day mentors for her. Over the next year, these women met with our daughter and let her shadow them for a day. They let her watch them at work, at home or on a trip. During that day, each of them shared with Bethany a "life message" God had given them for her.

What happened was amazing. These women took our idea to a whole new level. Sara, a nurse, knew that Bethany was considering becoming a nurse, as well. So she took her to a hospital maternity ward and the two of them spent the day helping mothers give birth to babies. That afternoon, Sara took Bethany to a class she taught for pregnant teens, many of them unwed mothers. At the close of the day, Sara's life message for Bethany revolved around sexual purity. (You can imagine that her message got through to Bethany much better than my lecture on the subject!)

Holly took Bethany on a one-day mission trip to urban Atlanta, where she worked with underprivileged kids who live in government housing. Betsy, a flight attendant, surprised Bethany by flying her up to New York City, months after the September 11th attacks. One after another, these ladies invested in our "little girl" one day at a time, for a year. They discussed topics like radical obedience to God, service and ministry, making your life an adventure and how to use her God-given influence for His purposes.

These women's voices still ring in Bethany's ears. Their messages weren't different than ours, but their voices were. And they confirmed God's love and calling in our daughter's life. Over the year, we noticed Bethany gaining confidence. She became secure when making difficult choices and experienced an increasing influence with her peers. We believe God used this community of believers to solidify our values in the home.

At the end of the year, we brought these six women together for an evening of blessing. You can read about it in the final section of this book. The night brought the mentoring process to a climax for Bethany. The evening had "teeth" to it, however, because of the experiences that occurred during the year.

Building Character and Discipline

It's Good For You

Sit down and discuss the things you and your young person really don't like doing. It may be a habit like sweeping the garage or some other chore around the house. It may be listening to or interacting with someone who seems unloveable. It may be physical exercise or the discipline of waiting. It could even be eating a vegetable you don't like.

Choose two of these "undesirables" and make them disciplines. Deliberately do what you don't like doing. Practice them daily for one week. Put them down on the calendar and hold each other accountable to do them. (If you do them for two weeks, chances are they will become a good habit!)

Afterward, discuss the results. Did you feel a sense of accomplishment? Did you waver in your commitment? Talk about how daily disciplines pave the way for conquering laziness and indifference. Look up I Corinthians 9:24-27. How have you gained a personal victory by practicing these disciplines?

Walk Through a Graveyard

At sunrise or sunset one day, drive out to a local graveyard. If you can, find an old one, where the gravestones have descriptions on them of the people who are buried there. Walk through the property, reading the epitaphs of each one you pass.

Afterward, sit down and discuss what you saw. Think about the lives of those who are described on those gravestones. Then, talk about the future. What kind of person does your young person want to be, as an adult? What do they want to accomplish before they die? What will be their values? Their purpose? Their methods? What are their motives?

Take a few minutes and journal these thoughts on paper. Consider Jesus' words at the end of His time on earth: "Father, I have glorified you on earth, having accomplished the purpose you have given me to do (John 17:4)." A few chapters later, Jesus said, "As the Father has sent Me, I also send you (John 20:21)." We have been given a mission to live for in the same way Jesus was.

Together, pray this prayer with King David: "Search me, O God, and know my heart; try me and know my anxious thoughts; And see if there be any hurtful way in me, and lead me in the everlasting way. (Psalm 139:23-24)."

Leadership Interview

Select a community leader who exhibits integrity and discipline. Set up an interview with them and ask them how they built that discipline in their life. Ask them how they determined to live with integrity, and how they stick to it, when it is difficult. Ask them how they failed along the way, and how they eventually gained victory over their flesh. Write down their answers and review them on the way home.

Finally, think about how you can follow the challenge of Hebrews 13:7: "Remember those who led you, who spoke the word of God to you; and considering the result of their conduct, imitate their faith."

Promises, Promises

Sit down and try to remember some promises you and your young person have made in the past. Make a list of them, and be sure and include some you failed to keep.

Next, select one of those unkept promises (to yourself or to someone else), and determine to keep that promise for one whole week. Fix your eyes on it as a clear goal. Write it down, and help each other think of steps you can take to keep the promise. Hold each other accountable. Write notes to each other; remind each other daily.

At the end of the week, talk it over. What does keeping a promise do to your sense of integrity? How does it positively affect your character? Does it strengthen your discipline? Now discuss Ecclesiastes 5:4-5: *When you make a vow to God, do not be late in paying it, for He takes no delight in fools. Pay what you vow! It is better that you should not vow than that you should vow and not pay.*

What's Behind the Commands

Together with your young person, find seven commands in the Bible. Select commands that God gave us in both the Old Testament and the New Testament. Write them down.

Now, discuss why God might have given them to us. What were His purposes behind telling us to do, or not to do, those things? Next to each of the seven commands you wrote down, write out your answers to the "why" question.

Finally, talk about how knowing why God commands something can help you obey it a little easier. Meaning fosters motion. Begin to see the benefits behind God's commands, and you will find that personal discipline comes easier.

Building Vision and Creativity

Bag of Vision

Fill a bag with several strange, unrelated items from around the house. The more weird the items are the better. Then, have each family member reach in the bag and pull one out. Give them a minute to think about it, then have them tell an imaginary story about the item—perhaps how it originated. Afterward, have them share a practical use for the item they've chosen, for which it was not originally designed. The item should solve a problem or address a human need in some way. Allow vision and creativity to flow.

After this crazy little exercise, talk about the importance of vision and creativity. How is being creative like God? What role does our imagination play as we come up with new ideas to solve problems? Why did God give us the ability to be creative and have vision?

Our imaginations can be used for good or bad purposes. Either way, they are powerful. Read Genesis 11:6: "And the Lord said, 'Behold, these people are all unified, working together with the same language...and now nothing they imagine to do will be impossible for them.'"

Pick Up Your Burden

Sit down with your young person, and talk about their school. What's happening on their campus? Once you get the conversation going, ask them to name one problem at their school that really needs to be solved.

Challenge them to "adopt" that problem as their own burden. Have them make a list of steps that could be taken to solve the problem. (These may be imaginary steps depending on the size of the burden they have chosen). Get them thinking about their vision for helping make the school a better place instead of complaining about how bad it is.

Finally, have them write about, draw a picture or clip out photos from magazines that depict the vision they have for their school. Have them create a mural if they wish. Then, post these pictures in their room as a reminder to both pray and act on their vision.

"Where there is no vision, the people are unrestrained, but happy is he who keeps the law (Proverbs 29:18)." What does this verse teach us about the power of a vision?

Building Vision and Creativity

Spin the Globe

Gather around your family globe. Talk about the different needs people have around the world. Ask your young person spin the globe, and have them point to a certain spot on it, as it revolves. When it finally stops, identify what country their finger is pointing.

Then, discuss the culture, the people and the needs of that nation. If you need help, I suggest you pick up a copy of the book, Operation: World, by Patrick Johnstone. The book is an encyclopedia of each country, giving commentary on how to pray for each one. Finally, decide what one thing you could do to help the country you've discussed. At the very least, pray for them and the needs they have. Add them to your prayer list for the week, or pick a new country each evening to pray for.

Read Psalm 67. Discuss the message of the psalmist: God has blessed us as a means to an end. He blesses us, that all the nations of the earth may hear about him. We are to utilize the blessings God has given us to bless others.

Find a Historical Mentor

Select a biography of a great leader in the past. Find one about a man or woman who had a big vision, and accomplished something great for the world. Read the biography together, or at least a chapter from the book. You may want to pay your young person a good sum for reading the book—after all, they get paid for doing chores; why not pay them for feeding their mind and heart with inspiring stories?

After they are finished with their reading, discuss the highlights of the book. Ask them what they enjoyed most about the story. Ask them how that leader caught his or her vision to make a difference in the world. What enabled them to endure hardship and finally achieve their goal?

Close your conversation by reading Hebrews 11:13: "All these (people of faith) died, not having received the fulfillment of God's promises, but having seen them and welcomed them by faith…"

Creative Shopping

For dinner one night, assign each of your young people one food item to shop for. Give them some money, and send them to the grocery store. Allow them to pick whatever they want to buy from a particular food group: protein, vegetable, fruit, dairy, starch, etc.

When they arrive home, examine the variety of items they have chosen. Then, give them permission to put on their creative thinking hats, and put together a great menu from what they have chosen. This will require both vision and creativity on their part. Help them only when it is necessary.

As you eat the meal, talk about their thinking process. How did they make the decisions on the menu? What was the most creative part of the meal? How did they get the ideas they came up with? Then, talk about what Jesus said in Luke 16:10: "He that is faithful with very little, will be faithful also in much; but he who is unfaithful in very little, will be unfaithful in much."

Building Relational Skills

Praying Through the Mall

Pick a time to take your young person to the shopping mall. Before leaving, tell them you are going to do an experiment that will help them learn to love and view people the way God does. (This experiment will be easier for older students).

Prepare them to walk alongside you as you stroll down the aisles of the mall. As you pass people, look into their eyes and observe their faces. Consider what kinds of needs those people are experiencing in their life. You'll find it's easy to spot loneliness on a face; it's easy to spot anger or aimlessness or depression.

As you pass them, smile at them. Then, once you've passed them, pray for the needs you might have seen in their faces. You might pray something as simple as: "Lord, those old folks looked lonely. Remind them of your presence, Lord, and if they don't know you, reveal yourself to them." Or, "Lord, those teenagers looked angry. Give them peace, Jesus, and if they don't know you, reveal yourself to them."

Do this experiment for as long as you want. I suggest you do it for about a half an hour. Afterward, sit down at a restaurant for a discussion. How did forcing yourself to stop, think about and pray about other's needs change your view of people? Remember Jesus did this too: "And when Jesus saw the multitudes, he felt compassion for them, because they were sheep without a shepherd..." (Matthew 9:36)

Be a Host

Visit the home of someone this week. Take your young person with you, and warn them to watch how well the person you visit hosts you, as guests. (You could also have them watch you, as you host guests in your own home.)

Afterward, talk about what it means to host others. A host is someone who takes initiative with others and makes them feel comfortable. They often guide the conversation, and do a lot of listening in the process. Then, explain that relational leaders are "hosts" in the relationships and conversations of their life. They are not guests, waiting for someone to tend to them.

Finally, have your young person practice hosting others this week. Have them focus on the needs and interests of others in conversations, not their own. Have them find one good quality about each person they meet and compliment them about it. Talk about how they are doing each night as you close out the day. Consider the scripture: "Love one another even as I have loved you..." (John 15:12).

How's Your Bedside Manner?

Pick a holiday coming up this month to celebrate. It doesn't have to be a big one. It could even be something like Ground Hog Day or St. Patrick's Day. Use it as an excuse to visit a hospital (or a children's hospital if you like), and celebrate the day with patients.

Gain permission from the hospital staff to walk through a floor on the hospital and visit each of the patients there. (Children's hospitals are great!) Take a small gift to them and get acquainted with each of them. Minister to them, as you discover their need for encouragement, listening, laughter or prayer. Use this opportunity to build your people skills with those you don't even know. Work at focusing on them, rather than yourself and your discomfort at being in a building full of sick people. Look for ways to serve them.

Afterward, discuss what you learned about people and people skills. What were some common discoveries you made about human nature? (i.e. we all like to be encouraged). What did you discover about yourself and your relational skills? Then, talk about what Jesus said in Matthew 20:25-28: "You know that the rulers of the Gentiles lord it over them, and their great men exercise authority over them. It is not so among you, but whoever wishes to become great among you shall be your servant, and whoever wishes to be first among you shall be your slave; just as the Son of Man did not come to be served, but to serve, and to give His life a ransom for many."

Love the One You Don't Like

Sit down together and talk about people who are difficult to be around—people who you don't connect with easily. (You might even be so bold as to say you just don't like them). Then, each of you choose one of these people to focus on this week.

Each day, direct your attention to them, but don't announce what you're doing to anyone. You may want to begin with conversation, giving them your undivided attention. Later, you may write them a note, affirming any good qualities you see in them. Perhaps you can do something to serve them and meet a need in their life. Maybe in give them a gift. The key is to do something that demonstrates love each day.

At the end of the week, talk about how you did. Was it hard? What made it difficult? How did the experience stretch you in your relational skills? Then, discuss Jesus' words in Matthew 25:31-46. Zero in on the passage: "Truly I say to you, to the extent that you did it to one of these brothers of Mine, even the least of them, you did it to Me."

If you prefer, focus on the passage: "If someone says, 'I love God,' and hates his brother, he is a liar; for the one who does not love his brother whom he has seen, cannot love God whom he has not seen." (I John 4:20)

People Skills Test

This idea can be done in a variety of ways. On a vacation or outing with your young person, tell them you are going to give them a "test" on their people skills afterward. Prepare them to interact with others while on the trip—even a simple trip to a restaurant where you talk with a waitress. Don't tell them what the quiz questions will be, but just prepare them to be ready to evaluate their experience when it's over.

When you are finished, sit down and give them the quiz. For example, after a meal at a restaurant, you may want to ask them: Did you remember the waitress' name? What was it? Did you show interest in her personal life? Did you ask about her family? Did you leave her with a word of encouragement? Talk over questions like this. Being aware of these issues will eventually build good habits in relationships.

Evaluate your experience against Colossians 4:5-6: "Conduct yourselves with wisdom toward outsiders, making the most of your opportunity. Let your speech always be with grace, seasoned as it were with salt, so that you may know how you should respond to each person."

Building
Planning Skills

Event Planning

Choose an event that would normally be planned by an adult. It is preferable that the event be something on the calendar each year. Instead of planning it yourself, ask your young person to do all the preparation. For instance, if you have a pet, let your young person make arrangements for pet care while you are out of town. If you don't, perhaps you can allow your young person to plan their own birthday party, given parameters of time, budget, and number of people who can attend. Depending on their age, check on them periodically, to make sure they stay on track and get answers to their questions. Allow them to follow through all the way to the completion of the event.

When it is over, discuss what happened. Have them read Nehemiah, chapters 1 – 3. Discuss how Nehemiah was given a project by God to accomplish, which required detailed planning. He and a team of workers rebuilt the wall around Jerusalem in record time: 52 days, because of his preparation. Talk about how God-given ideas and vision doesn't negate the necessity for planning.

Cash for Clothes

At the beginning of a new semester of school, sit down with your young person and discuss how much money you might normally spend on clothes for them. Once you arrive at a figure, tell them things will be different this semester. Give them the sum of money you agreed upon, and tell them they can have control of their clothes budget. They can get whatever they want, but that's all the money they will receive for the semester.

Talk about how they must assess their needs, and plan on distributing the money between what they want and what they need. The decision, however, is completely up to them. If they choose to "shoot their wad" on a nice coat, that's fine. They will just have to wear the same clothes the rest of the semester.

During or after their spending experience, sit down and talk about Proverbs 6:6-11. In this passage, we read about the tiny ant, who, although he is the smallest of creatures, plans and prepares for the future, and maintains a good attitude along the way. The ant needs no one to tell him what to do, because of his predisposition to plan and work hard.

Map Quest

Before taking a long trip or vacation, grab a map and ask your young person to plan the entire road trip. Talk them through the details, if necessary, but give them as much responsibility as you think appropriate. For instance, if you take a vacation, talk about how many days you will take to drive to your destination, where you'll need to refuel, eat and stay overnight, and even how much the trip might cost. Let them do the math and prepare the details of the trip.

Just before or just after the journey, sit down and discuss Luke 14:28-32. In this passage, Jesus spoke of the necessity of planning. He suggested it was unwise to begin anything without counting the cost, and seeing if you have the resources to get to your goal. Ask your young person what factors went into the planning of your road trip and how they calculated the stops along the way.

Building Planning Skills

A Game Without Goals

This idea works especially well if your young person enjoys sports. Attend a ballgame of any kind—football, baseball, hockey, soccer or basketball. Enjoy the game together.

Afterward, have a discussion at a restaurant. Have them imagine for a moment what that game might have been like had their not been any goals. How long would the game have lasted if the football field had not end zone; if the basketball court had no basketball, if the soccer field had no goal, etc? Have fun for a few minutes talking about how ridiculous sports would be without a goal. There would be no point. No one would come.

Then focus on their life for a moment. Life is just like sports in this way. There is no point without a goal, a mission. There would be no fulfillment. Perhaps this is why so many go to work everyday yet have no joy, and why they can come home, change their clothes and go play on a softball team—and have all kinds of energy for the game. At work they're unaware of the goal. Next, ask them what their goals are in life. Ask them what steps they are taking toward them. Finally, talk about Paul's words in Philippians 3:13-14. What was his goal? How did he glorify God?

Planning Their Financial Future

Over dinner sometime, discuss a big financial goal with your young person. Is there something really big they'd like to purchase? Is their something they want to invest in? Is there anything they are presently saving money for?

Once they come with something they really want, determine to plan how they can best save enough money for it, and how much time it will take. Factor in allowances, and any special project they may undertake to earn some extra money. Also factor in money they should give to the Lord and other necessities. Help them to focus on this goal, and not give in to the temptation to squander their money on other things, outside of their plan. Make this a project.

Once they achieve their goal, or when they give in to temptations, stop and discuss Matthew 7:24-27. Jesus told a story about a wise and foolish builder. What was the difference between wisdom and foolishness in His story? What is the lesson we can draw from it today?

Building Problem-Solving Skills

Choose a Crisis

Sit down and watch the news on television together, with a notepad in hand. Before the telecast, ask your young person to choose one crisis or problem reported in the news. If you prefer, read through the newspaper together. (There will be several stories in every newspaper or broadcast!) Once they choose the crisis, have them write down all the details you both can remember from the report. Then, pose this question to them: If you were in charge of this problem, what would you do to solve it? Ask them to assume leadership in their imagination, and jot down what steps they would take to remedy the crisis, from start to finish.

Evaluate their steps when they are finished. Did they leave anything out? Is their solution realistic? How expensive would it be? Did they diagnose the problem accurately? Look at how Jesus experienced this process in Matthew 9:35-10:8. His first step was embracing a burden for a problem; His next step was gaining vision for a solution; and finally He worked toward the fulfillment of that vision. Are there any steps your young person could actually take to implement their solution?

Watch a Movie

Check out the local movie listings to see if there are any movies showing where the plot involves solving a problem. You will notice that often a majority of the plots involve a dilemma that the lead character must resolve. Pick a good one, and go see it with your young person. Prepare them for a discussion afterward, over some dessert.

Discuss the story in detail. What was the problem? Why was it a problem? Who solved it? What did they do? Was it the best solution? Talk about how Jesus came to solve problems. Discuss the idea that all real leadership is about solving a problem. Pray about what problems lie in your young person's life that God may want them to help solve.

Visit an Amusement Park

Visit an amusement park together, with your young person. (It may be difficult to imagine visiting an amusement park without them!) Tell them as you enter the park that your goal is to have fun, but to also learn something. Prepare them to look for ways the amusement park could improve. Ask them to look for problems. Perhaps the customer service could be better. Maybe the lines for the rides require people to wait too long. It could be the restrooms are dirty or too hard to find.

At dinner time, after you've had plenty of time to spot problems, discuss them. Where were the places that ought to improve? Then, have your young person suggest ideas on how the park could make them better. Consider how pleasing it is to God when we are not satisfied with "good enough." Talk about King David's desire to build a Temple, because the tabernacle wasn't sufficient for His magnificent God. (II Samuel 7). Pray for God to give you an eye to see what could be better and what you could do to improve it.

Read All About It

Choose a leadership book that you and your young person can read. Over the next week, select what chapters you each will read, or choose to read the whole book, if possible. Optimally, the leadership book will specifically discuss problem solving. One suggestion might be *Developing the Leader Within You*, by John Maxwell, if your young person is age 15 or older. If they are in Middle School, you might try *Leading From the Lockers*, also by John Maxwell. In these books, you'll find a chapter on problem solving. When you have read it, discuss your personal application to the principles taught in the book. Identify a biblical truth and obey it. Find a place and time this week you each can practice what you learn.

This is based on James 1:26 where we are told to be "doers" of the Word, not merely hearers, who delude ourselves. Put action to the instruction. For more ideas on books to read, check out the Growing Leaders website, at: www.growingleaders.com.

Act It Out

Sometime when you're together, come up with a challenge that you and your young person believe is a legitimate problem in your school or community. Talk about it, then discuss possible solutions. Then, narrow it down to one. Finally, choose an evening when both of you act it out together, (the problem and solution) before friends or family members. You might make it like a game of charades, where those watching try to figure out what you are doing, and what problem you are trying to solve.

Later, when you are alone again, check out Ezra 7:10. In this passage, we can see the correct order of learning: Ezra studied the law of God, then he practiced it, then he taught those statutes to Israel. Learn it. Do it. Pass it on. Talk about how you can pass on problem solving skills to others.

Building Values and Ethics

Lost and Found

Go to the shopping mall with your young person. As you window shop, secretly drop a $10 dollar bill on the floor, where they will see it. Make sure they do not know you are the source of the money. When either of you spot it, don't offer any suggestions to them on what to do. Allow them to reveal their heart. Will they keep it? Will they find a way to return it to the owner? Is it even possible to find the owner? Wouldn't everybody claim that it was their money? Within a few minutes, you and your young person will be ready to discuss what to do with your find.

Once he or she draws a conclusion, talk about how it reflects the personal values they've embraced. Proverbs 4:18-19 reminds us that the path of a good person is well lit, while the path of an evil person who has no values gets darker and darker. What kind of values have you both chosen to live by?

TV Lies

This one is fun. Watch TV some evening, or see a movie in which you know one of the characters has questionable values. Explain to your young person they are to watch the commercials or the show for the purpose of discussion. Either during or after the program, discuss how often you saw lies in the commercials, the program or the movie. How do commercials over-promise what they can deliver? Did you hear any outright lies? How did the characters in the movie or program display unhealthy values? Were they deceitful? If so, why were they?

Now discuss this. How do they reflect real life? How can you live out a counter culture in your home or school? Take a moment and read Romans 12:2: "Don't be conformed to this world, but be transformed by the renewing of your mind..." What does this mean?

The Hiding Place

I got this idea from a friend who's had great success with it. It will take a little preparation. Choose a night to talk about the people during World War Two who refused to cooperate with Nazi Germany, as they murdered millions of Jewish citizens in several countries. Talk about how many of them took their Jewish neighbors in and hid them in secret rooms or crawl spaces in their homes. Their efforts saved countless lives, even though it cost some of them their life, when the Nazis discovered these hiding places.

Next, simulate the experience in your own home. Pick a secret room in your basement, your attic or a crawl space under your home. If you can, play a tape or CD with the sound effects of bombs and gunfire, or perhaps a thunderstorm. Grab some flashlights and run to the hiding place you've selected. Tell your young people you have thirty seconds to get there, or you will be captured. You may even want to surprise your young people (if they are old enough to experience it), by having a neighbor come in and look for you, as if they were trying to capture you. Do this for as long as everyone seems to be engaged in the exercise.

Afterward, talk about the experience. How did you feel? Ask your young people: Is there anything you believe in so strongly that you would risk your life for it? The book of Revelation talks about the martyrs who will be rewarded in the end for their willingness to give their life for God's Kingdom. Hebrews 11:35-40 tells about how many of the Old Testament saints gave their lives by faith. Jesus, Himself, said: "He that wants to save his life, will lose it. He that loses his life for My sake, will save it (Mark 35)."

Stand For a Cause

Sit down with your young person and choose an organization that stands for a cause, and pray for them. The cause could be helping unwed mothers avoid abortion; it could be feeding the homeless, it could be building homes with Habitat for Humanity, or it could be cleaning up the roadsides in your community. Be sure and choose one you believe in.

Once you've prayed for them every day for a few days, pick a Saturday and go help them. Take a stand with them. Do something that communicates you believe in putting feet to your values. I John 3:17-18 reminds us that if we say we love our brother, but see him in need and do nothing about it, the love of God does not abide in us. Hmmm. Jesus said it in an even stronger way. He asked, "Why do you call me Lord, Lord and do not do what I say?" (Luke 6:46) Talk over what it really means to believe in something.

Memory Lane

Take out some old photos of you when you were growing up, and look them over with your young person. You might even want to get some hot chocolate and sit down with a photo album for an entire evening. Talk about some fun memories you had growing up. Talk about what was happening when the pictures were taken, years ago. Try to remember the pivotal moments when your life was shaped as a young person.

Next, begin to talk about the values your parents passed on to you. Discuss the ones you wish they would have given you, if you feel you didn't receive a strong foundation of values. Whenever possible, talk about what your parents did right, as they raised you.

Next, choose six core values that you and your young person believe would be good ones to embrace today. You may choose words as simple as honesty, service, or generosity. Grab a Bible if you wish, and look up scriptural bases for the values. Once you come up with your list, pray about how you can practice them.

52 Leadership Ideas

Building Courage and Risk-Taking Skills

Attempt the Impossible

This idea works best when both of you make the commitment and hold each other accountable to keep it. Sit down together and determine to attempt something this week you couldn't possibly pull off without God. It may be a big goal they set for school, or it could be taking the risk to talk to someone about your faith. Both you and your young person should share what you'll attempt this week, then pray for each other. The Lord may even lead you to attempt something you hadn't planned. The key is to step outside of your comfort zone. Share what happened at the end of the week.

The Apostle Paul was consistently attempting the impossible. He put himself in situations where God had to show up, or he was sunk. That's why God was so real to him. His goal wasn't survival—it was pleasing God. In Acts 20:24 he said he didn't even count his life as dear to him, so that he could finish his calling and ministry with joy. Pray for that same spirit in yourselves.

From Procrastination to Progress

This week, identify one personal goal you've procrastinated in fulfilling, one that you've never gotten around to achieving. Share it with your young person. Then, ask them to do the same thing. Talk about why we procrastinate and what role fear plays in the process. Once you discussed your unrealized goal, force yourselves to make a decision on it this week. Act on it in some way. Take a step toward fulfilling it. Once again, hold each other accountable to the step you say you are going to take.

Very often, procrastination is directly tied to fear. We wait on doing something because we are afraid of the outcome. We might fail. We might look stupid. We might not know what to do in the middle of the whole thing. So—we procrastinate. Sometimes the best remedy is one simple step of action.

Now look at Romans 13:11-12. Paul writes, "Do this, knowing the time, that now it is high time to awake out of sleep; for now our salvation is nearer to us than when we first believed. The night is far spent, the day is at hand..." Pray for each other to know what your one step of action should be.

Raising Cash and Courage

Sometimes the scariest thing for people to do is to raise money from people they don't know. It's a test of courage. That's what this little idea revolves around. Have your young person choose a charity they really believe in. If they don't know of any, check some out on the Internet. Then, go raise $500 from people you don't necessarily know, for this worthwhile organization. Make a list of those you can talk to, and what you'll say when you discuss the project. Then, take time this week to approach these people with your idea.

Jesus calls us to be extravagant in our giving, even to the point of taking risks. Generosity comes from a faith that God is able to supply our own needs. In Matthew 10:8 Jesus said: "Heal the sick, cleanse the lepers, raise the dead, cast out demons. Freely you have received, freely give." Does your courage come from trusting God?

Shadowing

Invite your young person to shadow you at work, one day. Choose a day where they can observe you in a variety of tasks, and where you can talk them through responsibilities you have on the job. For most young people, this kind of thing is very enlightening, and depending on how old they are, a little intimidating. Show them the relationship between responsibility and courage. Communicate how a person must step up and perform some difficult (even intimidating) tasks simply because they must be done. Show them the relationship between your conscience and your courage. Commitment breeds courage.

Afterward, discuss some biblical characters where commitment and courage were evident. You may want to start with Daniel (Daniel 6), or Shadrach, Meshach and Abednego (Daniel 3). Talk about how leaders feel responsible which leads them to do courageous things.

Taking Initiative

This idea has two options, depending on the age of your young person. If they are younger, go out to eat at a restaurant. Once you are seated, have your young person lead the discussion on what everyone wants to eat, then have them do all the ordering, when the waiter comes. (You might even ask your young person to remember the name of the waiter!) Through the dinner, have your young person take the initiative to care for all the needs— from refills on the drinks to ordering the dessert. This will require both initiative and courage.

If they are older, have them identify a person who exhibits courage and risk taking skills. Ask them to take initiative to set up an interview with them and ask them what gives them courage. You can go with them, but make sure your young person has a series of questions ready to ask and can take initiative on guiding the conversation.

Afterward, debrief your experience. Discuss what they learned. Talk about why God requires courage from leaders. Look up the story of Joshua, and notice what God said to him as he began his new leadership role: Joshua 1:6-9

52 Leadership Ideas

Building Teamwork and Servanthood

Feeding the Homeless

Locate a local homeless shelter or soup kitchen. Go together to the shelter and serve meals to the homeless. Be sure and get your young person involved in the process. Let them experience what it means to serve others, on a team of people.

Afterward, discuss how it made you feel. Describe your experience to one another: how did you feel about serving the needy? How about the sounds, the smells and the sights of it all? Did you feel uncomfortable? Is this where Jesus would be serving?

Why was it important to have a team of people serving? Could one person get the job done? Once you discuss the experience, pray about it. During your prayer time, check out Matthew 20:25 where Jesus reminds us that He came not to be served, but to serve and to give His life a ransom for many.

Family Work Day

Plan a family work-day, some Saturday. Assemble a team of people, or your entire family and go through closets to find clothes and other items that you don't need and that would be useful to the Salvation Army, or some other charity that provides for the needy. Make it a team effort, organizing items into boxes or bags. Include everyone in taking the items to the charity you have chosen as well. This will become a win/win/win: you get rid of things you don't need, the needy benefit, and you learn what it means to work as a team.

Afterward, take some time over pizza to discuss I Corinthians 12:4-7. In this passage, Paul talks about how Christians are like a body, working together, each contributing what they have to offer. Talk about the role each of your team (family) plays, and what the special contribution is that each one makes.

Work to Win

Prepare to hand out Saturday chores, some weekend. Ask each young person (if you have more than one) to do a list of chores that are appropriate for their age.

Without telling them, hide envelope with money in it or tickets to a ballgame, and put it where they'll find it if they do the chores very thoroughly. For instance, if you tell them to clean out the sofa—you may hide ten dollars under the cushions that they can find and keep if their work is thorough. Or, you may tell them to clean out their closet, and you can hide some tickets to a movie or ballgame—and they'll find them if they are thorough. The winner is the one who works with excellence. Hopefully, everyone will win.

Once everyone is finished, check out Ephesians 6:7-8. Paul tells us that whatever we do, we should do it as unto the Lord, not merely for people. How does our work reflect what we think about God? Pray about this one.

Mission Trip

This one will require you to plan ahead. Investigate mission opportunities that your church or some other ministry may be sponsoring locally. If possible, plan to go on a cross-cultural mission trip together and serve in some unfamiliar place, such as among Native American Indians or in Mexico. Make sure it's a place where you are out of your comfort zone, you have to trust God to see you through the day, and you are concentrating on serving others.

This kind of a ministry trip does wonderful things for those who participate. Once you return home, take some time to debrief the experience. How did you work together as a team? What was the highlight of the trip? How could the service you rendered on the trip become a lifestyle for you at home?

Look up John 13:1-15. It tells the story of Jesus serving His team of twelve men. After washing their feet that night, he told them that this was to be their lifestyle. He had given them an example that they should follow. Pray about making service a lifestyle.

Team Building

This activity may take different forms depending on the season of the year. For instance, in the fall, you may have leaves to rake in your yard. Why not ask your young person to rake leaves for you or for a needy person who lives nearby? Suggest that they organize a team to do the raking, and offer to pay them for their effort. Talk about how many people they'll need on the team and what's involved if they're going to do a good job. (If it's winter, you might have them shovel snow; if it's summer or spring they could wash cars.)

The key to this activity is preparation. Be sure and take the time to really discuss how your young person can make this project work. Get them organized. Whatever you are going to pay them, give the money to your young person to divide up between the team members. Let them experience what it means to be a supervisor and see the job through to the end.

Afterward, talk about the story of the tower of Babel in Genesis 11. Although the builders were acting apart from God's will, God affirms their teamwork. In verse 6, God says that nothing they plan to do shall be impossible when they work together.

52 Leadership Ideas

Building Communication Skills

Adult Interaction

Learning to communicate is inseparable from good leadership. The better we communicate, the better our chances are of becoming an effective leader. The good news is that young people can learn communication from the simplest situations.

For instance, the next time you host a party, ask your young person to help you serve the guests. Give them a job where they will have to interact with adults, such as overseeing the punch bowl, or taking coats, or passing out snack plates. Having a job will make conversation less awkward for them, yet it will get them mixing socially with adults.

Another idea to reach the same goal can take place the next time your young person is due for an appointment. Have your kids call to set up their appointments to see the dentist, to get a haircut, or to see the orthodontist. This will be easy for some temperaments, but challenging for others. However, anytime we have to communicate in order to accomplish a goal—it is good for us. Sit down with your young person afterward and talk about Ecclesiastes 12:11. Solomon writes that our words can be like "tools" to accomplish tasks. How is that so?

Writing Contests

Check with your local schools to see if there are any writing contests for young people to enter. The next time there's a contest, challenge your young person to enter it. Have them write on something they really care about—but encourage them to do it with excellence. Talk through the writing process with them and help them to get their point across in the most colorful and effective way possible.

Once the contest is over, talk about what they learned from it. Ask them what they understand about making a point clear and compelling. Then, read about how Nehemiah did it, in Nehemiah 1-2. Nehemiah was the king's cupbearer, but he felt he had to rebuild the broken walls around Jerusalem. Notice how he communicated with the king, and how he spoke with the potential helpers. How did he make his point and get them to join him?

Backyard Bible Club

During the spring or summer, sign up to host a Backyard Bible Club, or a Vacation Bible School at your house. There are a variety of these programs available and most churches do them at some point. This will not only give you an opportunity to minister to kids, but to allow your young person to help lead it.

Ask your young person to teach the younger kids, or to read the story each day. Give them a chance to communicate with others, and accomplish something in the process. After the week is over, talk about what they learned, from helping to lead it. Discuss how those who teach have a greater responsibility, and a greater impact on others. Read James 3:1 and talk about why he warned people to not take the role of communicating lightly. Then, read the next several verses about the power of our words. Pray that God will use yours for good.

Editorials

Sit down with your young person and read the editorial section of the newspaper. Talk about why newspapers include this section each day. After reading a couple of them, have your young person choose an issue they are interested in, and write an editorial of their own. They can keep it simple and short, but work with them to make it compelling. This may get them reading the editorials in the following days to see if theirs gets published!

During the process, talk about the power of words. Look up Proverbs 18:21. In this verse, Solomon informs us that death and life are in the power of the tongue! That's quite a statement. What do you suppose he means?

Role Reversal

This one is fun when you have two generations present. It is ideal for the family. Take some time one evening and play a game called: Role Reversal. This is where the adults and the young people switch roles—and learn some revealing lessons in the process.

Have the young people become parents, and deal with a young person who had just lied to them, or perhaps came home late one night. Encourage everyone to really step into the parts. This may take a little time, but try to get past the laughter and consider what both generations are experiencing. Think of at least three tough situations you might experience in real life, and play the role reversal game. Afterward, take the time to discuss what each person felt. How did communication take on new forms, when the roles were changed?

Now look at Matthew 7:3-5. Jesus warned us to take the log out of our own eye before we both to take the speck out of our brothers. He also taught the golden rule: Do unto others as you would have them do unto you. Talk about what this means for your communication.

Building Identity
and
Self-Esteem

Who They Are in Christ

This is an interesting Bible study you can do over a period of one or two weeks. Study the passages of scripture in the New Testament (letters of Paul) where he uses the terms: "in Christ, in Him, or with Him." Whenever he used those terms, he was describing our new identity in Christ. We are new creatures in Christ Jesus (II Corinthians 5:17). Paul intended for Christians to live on the basis of their new position in Christ, not based on their up and down experience in this world. Our identity should be drawn from who God says we are. Here is a start on your study: II Corinthians 5:17-21, Ephesians 1:18-23, Romans 8:1, I Corinthians 1:30, Ephesians 4:7.

Once you've noted the references that use these terms, draw a diagram that shows these qualities inside of you. Outline your own body, then write in the truths you learn from the scriptures on who you are in Christ. Put this little diagram up on your bathroom mirror and look at it every day. Allow it to shape your self esteem.

Brag on Them

This one is simple, but could have a memorable effect on your young person. Find three adults this week, and spend time with them along with your young person. At a natural, appropriate time, brag to them about your young person, in front of them. Don't make it syrupy or unbelievable, but simply affirm the gifts or strengths or qualities your young person possesses, in front of them. Few things have a more lasting effect than for a young person to listen in on adult conversation, especially if it pertains to them. The conversations I remember most growing up were not ones between me and an adult, but between two adults when I was eavesdropping. When we are growing up, a good part of our self esteem is derived from what those we respect think of us. This is your chance to build the esteem of your young person by talking positively about them in their presence.

Proverbs 27:2 states we're to let another man praise us rather than praising ourselves. This passage has a double value. Not only does it promotes humility, but it encourages us to affirm one another. I believe we as adults can use this to build the next generation.

Building Identity and Self-Esteem

Hanging Out with Giants

Take some time to discuss some great leaders of the past, with our young person. Ask them about some of their heroes who might be considered good leaders. Pay your young person money to read biography of one of these favorite leaders who accomplished great feats. In fact, you may want to read the same book together. Later, take time to discuss what you learn from the leader. What were some highlights about their life? What enable them to achieve what they did, or excel above their peers? What did you both identify with in their life? What can you do today, that you learned from reading about their life?

The Apostle Paul reminds us, in I Corinthians 10:11, that past events occurred for our benefit; that we are to learn from their successes and failures. Biographies create mentors out of former leaders that we can learn from.

Identity Their Gift

This exercise is key for building both a sense of identity and some leadership direction for your young person. Take some time to focus on your young person's strengths: their natural talents, their spiritual gifts, and their acquired skills. Discuss the issue with them. Make a list of the strengths that fit into each of these three categories.

After you've helped your young person identify their primary gift(s), focus your attention on developing that gift or talent. For instance, if they possess word gifts or a talent for speaking or writing, direct them to enroll in speech class or to audition for a play. If they are good at organizing things, help them find a leadership role or a student government position that would allow them to groom that gift. In other words, find a match for their gift and a role. I believe that when young people find their strength, then choose to serve in the area of their strength—they will naturally find themselves leading in that area eventually. Influence grows out of personal gifts. Proverbs 18:16 teaches us: "A man's gift makes room for him and brings him before great men."

Say I Love You

This week, make a point to say "I love you" and hug your young person daily, even if they are in the "too cool to hug back" stage. Don't worry about their response or lack of response. Initiate the act of affirming your love for them and their value to the group, or the team or the family they are part of. Nothing improves a person's sense of worth than being reminded of how much they are loved and valued by others.

I John 4:18 reminds us there is no fear in love, but perfect love casts out fear. Our greatest sense of security comes from unconditional love. When we have it, we don't fear rejection or judgment or failure. Few gifts prepare us to lead others than to know assuredly that we are loved and valued for who we are. Young people can perform at their best when there is a foundation of love and grace beneath them.

Confirming the Blessing

Confirming the Blessing

In the beginning of this little book, I shared the story of my daughter Bethany and her thirteenth year. During that year, my wife and I, along with Bethany, selected six women that we admired and respected, and asked them to be one-day mentors for our little girl. Each of these ladies spoke into her life and shared a "life message" with Bethany during the day they had together. Some of them went on trips, some allowed Bethany to shadow them at work, others just spent a fun day together sharing in a safe conversation some values they wanted to pass on to her. Needless to say, it made a lasting impression on her.

The year came to a climax, when we invited all six of these mentors to our home for a dinner party. We had four objectives at this party. First, we wanted these godly women to meet each other and see the others who were participating in this special year. Second, we wanted to say thank you for their investment in our daughter. Third, we wanted Bethany to have a chance at the end of the year to share with them what the lasting lessons were she learned from them, as they spent time together. Finally, we wanted to spend the evening offering a blessing to Bethany—not only from mom and dad, but from six older females who were models of the kind of life she wanted to live as she grew into adulthood.

Dinner time was a fun time of sharing. Many of the ladies did not know each other, and only had Bethany as a common ground at first. It was a great time for Bethany to sit down again with adults and host conversation with adults. Following dinner, we moved into our family room, where Bethany took some cards out. On the cards, she had written personal thank you notes to these women, sharing specific things she had learned from each of them. It was a meaningful time for the women, but especially good for Bethany who had to put into words the value she had gained from their lives.

When Bethany was finished, I shared briefly with the women the concept of "the blessing." In the Old Testament, fathers would bless their sons. They would speak words of affirmation to them, words of encouragement about their future, and even issue words of direction and caution on this special occasion, they called the blessing. I then invited these women (who had already blessed our daughter by spending time with her) to speak a word of blessing over her. Although I told them their was no obligation to contrive something if they didn't have anything more to share—

they immediately jumped in. Over the next thirty minutes, each of them spoke directly to Bethany. They told her what they saw in her, and the potential they believed she possessed. They warned her about what to watch out for during her high school and college years. They reminded her of the gifts she had inside, and to not waste what God had given her. They shared with her the beauty they could see both inside and out. It was a moving time.

The evening ended with these women gathering around Bethany to lay hands on her, and to pray for her and for her future. Each of them prayed through tears, as they recognized the significance of the occasion to a young teen.

As they left that night, Bethany presented them with a gift, once again to express our thanks to them for such a valuable investment in her young life. The year and that particular night accomplished everything we hoped it would, as we planned it months before. I had to laugh as I tucked my young son, Jonathan, into bed that night. Crawling under the covers, he told me: "Dad, I already know the six guys I want to mentor me when I turn thirteen."

I love to create hunger in young people to reach high and become everything God intended for them to be. I have the privilege of doing this not only with my two children, but with thousands of students across the country every year. And you do, too, with the young people right under your nose. It's one of the highest aims we can strive for. Don't allow survival to become your goal. Don't let mere maintenance satisfy you. Look deep inside of those students with whom you work. There's gold inside of them. They have influence—every one of them. Help them uncover the "salt and light" God placed in them, so that they could influence their world. It begins with you and a handful of simple ideas.

Ready to Start Growing Leaders?

If you are passionate about raising up leaders, we encourage you to find the suitable resources on our website. We've developed leadership books, tapes, videos, and mentoring group guides to build emerging leaders. See for yourself—visit www.growingleaders.com.

Featured Resources

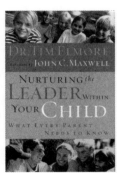

Nurturing the Leader Withing Your Child
By Tim Elmore
A handbook to leadership training for teachers, parents, and youth pastors, *Nurturing the Leader Within Your Child* provides you with dynamic development and assessment tools for bringing out the leader in your child. Offering step-by-step instruction and suggestions, Tim Elmore examines such critical topics as:

- How to connect with your Kid
- Seizing the Teachable Moments
- Mentoring Your Child to Become a Leader

Other adult resources by Tim Elmore include:
- *The Greatest Mentors in the Bible* • *Soul Provider*
- *Pivotal Praying (w/ John Hull)* • *Leaders Everywhere (w/ Art Fuller)*

Authentic Influence: Leading Without Titles
By Tim Elmore   Ages 16-24
Other titles in this series include:
Wired for Influence: Skills to Lead Others
Intentional Influence: Investing Your Life Through Mentoring
Leveraging Your Influence: Impacting Your Students for Christ

Leading from the Lockers
By John C. Maxwell   Ages 10-13
Also check out the companion Power Pak series:
Leading as a Friend
Leading on your Sports Team
Leading at School
Leading in Your Youth Group

To purchase these and other resources available from
Growing Leaders, visit
www.growingleaders.com